A GREAT VALLEY UNDER THE STARS

SELECTED TRANSLATIONS AND STUDIES BY ROYALL TYLER:

Pining Wind: A Cycle of Nō Plays
Granny Mountains: A Second Cycle of Nō Plays
Japanese Tales
French Folktales
Japanese Nō Dramas
The Miracles of the Kasuga Deity
The Tale of Genji
Matsutarō Kawaguchi, *Mistress Oriku: Stories from a Tokyo Teahouse*
Shōtarō Yasuoka, *The Glass Slipper and Other Stories*
The Ise Stories: Ise Monogatari (with Joshua Mostow)
Takehiko Fukunaga, *Flowers of Grass*
The Tale of the Heike
Before Heike *and After:* Hōgen, Heiji, Jōkyūki
To Hallow Genji: A Tribute to Nō
A Reading of The Tale of Genji

A GREAT VALLEY UNDER THE STARS

Royall Tyler

ISOBAR
PRESS

First published in 2014 by

Isobar Press
Sakura 2-21-23-202
Setagaya-ku
Tokyo 156-0053
Japan

http://isobarpress.com

ISBN 978-4-907359-05-8

© Royall Tyler, 2014
All rights reserved.

ACKNOWLEDGEMENTS

Cover photo:
'Portal Peak in the Chiricahua Mountains'
by BAlvarius (http://commons.wikimedia.org).

Frontispiece (page 7):
'Mouser Canyon, Peloncillo Mountains, New Mexico'
by BAlvarius; used by permission.

CONTENTS

Rodeo	11
The Shady Grove	12
Song of the One Who Stands in the Doorway	14
Song of the Two-Eyed Stranger	15
Notes from The Shady Grove	19
Notes from Rodeo	27
From a Wintry Northern State	33

A Great Valley Under the Stars

Rodeo

Back then I lived in Rodeo, New Mexico, up against the Arizona line. Population: 75 or so. The long valley was miles wide. The land unit was the section: 640 acres.

From Rodeo the ground sloped up to the Peloncillos. Over in Arizona rose the lofty Chiricahuas, crowned by Portal Peak.

Adeline ran the post office. The talk there was about rain: how much, how long it had been, whether we would ever get any. There was a bar, which I never entered. A broken-down Conoco gas station and a dingy Enco station served local and passing traffic. Fifty miles up the road: Lordsburg, New Mexico. Fifty miles down the road: Douglas, Arizona. That was about it. Otherwise, mesquite, catclaw acacia, ephedra, yucca, agave, barrel cactus, coyotes, and jackrabbits; and, up in the Peloncillos, javelinas and rumored mountain lions. Ranchers drove pickups with a rifle rack fixed across the rear window.

Adeline and Bill lived far up a canyon. Once they adopted an orphan baby mountain lion. Great fun, but baby grew. One day Adeline was carrying a big basket of washing back from the line when the playful mountain lion jumped into it and knocked her flat.

The Shady Grove

For six months I worked twelve-hour shifts at a truckstop up on the Interstate, toward Lordsburg – a big operation, alone in the desert. There wasn't a tree in sight. It was called the Shady Grove.

The Shady Grove ancestors were an old couple. They presided over the place like Adam and Eve. Old Eve reigned over the café run by her two daughters; old Adam lorded it over the truck refueling and repair section run by his two sons-in-law.

So one side of the Shady Grove was male, the other female. The food side was the best in the county. The fuel side sold vast quantities of diesel. The two had no visible commerce with each other. The women never appeared on the men's side, and if the men ate in the café, they paid for their meals like anyone else. One building housed both. A glass door stood between them like the twilight zone between worlds.

Only one Shady Grove employee worked for both sides at once: the janitor, me. I was, in each realm, the inevitable mote from the other.

My chief duties were to clean the toilets and to remove the garbage from the café. The men's opened off the truckers' shop area, but the women's was accessible only from outside. I loaded the big garbage cans onto a trailer behind a coughing pickup truck and hauled them half a mile or so over the desert to the dump. This was a huge trench. Into it I dumped the garbage and any other trash, poured gasoline over it all, and dropped in a match. *Poom*! The aerosol cans leapt high in the air as they exploded.

My sanctum was the men's room. I rigged up a sort of standup desk in there, in the supply closet. Truckers coming back through the Shady Grove on their return run would find me in the same position they had seen me in last time, reading Japanese poetry. This puzzled some of them.

The Ōmine range, Yoshino down to Kumano, is set up just like the Shady Grove. The Yoshino half is the Diamond Realm mandala and the southern, Kumano half the Womb Realm. They touch at a narrow saddle. I once camped there. Nameless beings thumped and crackled around the tent.

Song of the One Who Stands in the Doorway

There is a far off land
quite close, beyond the glass,
fair in the moonlight,
scented with flowers not rare
but exquisite, alive
with song;

There is a nearby land
far off, within the blood,
taut with terror,
caught in the glare of fires,
foul with the stench of strange things burning,
shrieking mute.

Song of the Two-Eyed Stranger

Let sun and moon stand together
when with the lamb the lion
lies on the green field
at peace, in place,
and tangible, O Lord,
above all, to the touch,
firm and warm.

Notes from The Shady Grove

First thing in the morning, in the warm, cluttered, bare bulb-lit storeroom, filling soap dispensers from the big drum – funny how the mind turns to Vermont, to the places the Appalachian Trail guidebook calls 'beaver activity': a swampy pond with dark, calm waters, surface everywhere broken by gaunt grey skeletons of trees; and the trail winding by amidst the green.

❧

It's amazing, and touching, too, how those little sparrows build nests up in the steel beams of the service area roof, right over the pumps where the trucks pull in. Those exhaust pipes reach almost to the nests, belching engine wastes. But the birds make out. When the drive is empty you can see and hear them, flittering around up there. They look so out of place. Any organic matter beside truckers, paper, and, say, candy bars – especially if it's alive – looks odd in a truckstop. An occasional fly in the men's room looks like an infection from outer space, and a cricket might as well be on the moon. Sometimes small, anonymous moths show up in the lobby but for whatever reason they die after fluttering around in weak circles on the floor and get swept up with the trash.

This morning I'd just cleaned the ladies' room, and when I came out, there was a sparrow, making little, short flights, very low, around on the drive. He paused on the cement by the lobby wall, and I went toward him: ragged tail feathers, and he was breathing hard. I thought he must be sick, but he was still lively enough to escape. He took off, flew under a parked truck, and disappeared.

❧

> Oh Shenandoah, I love your daughter,
> Oh, away, my rolling river.
> She lives across your stormy waters.

Weigh hey, we're bound away
'Cross the wide Missouri.

❧

Rays of the sun, new-risen, gleam gold on the Timex watch display, the bumper sticker rack; splash pools of light over the pump islands and the drive. Red & Sandy head home, hand in hand. Parked trucks are silent. Drivers wander in the clear, cool air, uncertain where they are, or when. A woman climbs back in a cab. Truckstop morning.

❧

Little birds cheeping on the roof, I hear them through the cooler vent. They sound like gulls. How did the sea get here today?

❧

Just look at their feet. Every one wears western boots – some plain, polished, some battered & scraped, some fancy two-tone with snakeskin (fake?) trim, some with sculptured brass toes and heels. The manly life. Sitting hour after hour on their butts, at their tame monster's wheel, from rest stop to rest stop where the waitresses mother them or wiggle at them, depending on age. CB radio, a new antenna, silly decals & knick-knacks, shower and wash up, coffee. Not much left of the cowboy.

No, that's not what I meant to say. I don't know what I meant to say. I don't know these men. Commerce rolls on their wheels. Their banner, though: a grinning girl, bare-waisted, posturing beside the glossy photo of a new, heavy truck. Roaring engines and pussy.

❧

'Pour être inscrit au Guide Michelin, pas de piston, pas de pot de vin.'

If you want a good piece of ass,
see fat Linda in the café,

says the men's room wall.

≥●

I had him picked out from the start as a zombie, servicing the trucks out on the drive. A deadness to his blank face, something of wooden self-preoccupation in his carriage. Chuck. He told me not long ago he was from New York, likes to go back there when he can. He's got an application in at the New School for this fall. Oh. An intellectually-inclined zombie, then.

Today he comes up to me. 'Hey, I hear you've published things.' 'Yeah.' 'What kind of writing so you do?' 'I translate from Japanese, mostly' 'That's my bag, too, writing.' 'Oh yeah? Had anything published?' 'A few things.' 'What? Poetry?' 'Well, a little – don't do too well with poetry, though. Heh, heh, I'd like to, but…' 'What do you usually write, then?' 'Well, you know, Kerouac, Ginsberg, stuff like that… That's what I go for.' 'Yeah? So you write novels?' 'It's kind of like Kerouac, Ginsberg, you know… Free form, no rigid framework…' A truck pulls in, he fades out to refuel it.

A literary zombie, even.

≥●

Thinking of Fudō. Glimpses of deep red & more deep green, feeling of freshness, smell of pines. A noble forest out there somewhere. Looking forward to finding it, walking in: a path in here somewhere to the king of trees.

Propter magnam gloriam tuam
we magnify, we glorify Thy name –
> Thy name? Thy name?
Do we know Thy name?
> 'Oh yes,' she said, 'God does have many names, but Krishna is his original name. Krishna is blue, he wears certain ornaments, etc. What other religion tells you exactly what the Supreme Personality of Godhead looks like?'

❧

A bit of old toilet paper, caught in dry tumbleweed.
Choiring waves of bare desert hills, blue-shadowed, like light.
Walking along, tending the garbage fires.
Tender breeze, as of the sea.

❧

(Overheard at the cashier's counter)
'Could I have some matches, please?'
'Watcha wanna do with all those matches? Set the world on fire?'
'Sure! You bet! Just a buncha trash anyway!'

❧

Trashman sings:

> O plastic bags bulging with squashy masses,
> (Oops! It split! Coffee grounds tumble and spill)
> Stale buns by the sackful, soon to be ashes,
> Tin cans all drippy and sticky with swill;

>   Potato peels, fat, soggy napkins and boxes
>   Long or flat, flimsy or sturdy, all kinds,
>   Beer cans and pop cans, cans that go bang,
>   Sweepings and cigarette butts, melon rinds.

(Damn that howling wind, hot & dusty – whooshing the dust, wheeing the wires strung over the dump. Hot grit. June's too late for this!)

>   Disposable diapers, feminine napkins (used),
>   Oily rags, blown-out tires large and small,
>   Broken display racks...

(Doggone that Delbert, where'd he leave the truck?)

❦

I wonder why the first urinal in line, nearest the door, gets so much more traffic than the others, while you can never tell which stall a man will use. No one (except Al & Bob & John, who always hit the third) ever uses any urinal but the first, unless it's already in use. But most men sniff around for the right place to dump their load. Occult considerations.

❦

A sign to post in the men's stalls:
>   For Pete's sake don't put your feet up on the seat. How would you like to sit on black smudges? I can't be everywhere at once.
>
>   The Janitor

❦

(The trucking life)
>'Boy, I wish I could learn how to drive a truck side-saddle, so I could get my other arm suntanned!'

                                ک

A fruit, time after time eagerly bitten into, that always proves hard, unripe:
>you could say that of the Three Worlds,
>you could say it of almost anything
>you hold too close, I guess.

My goodness! *The Jewel Ornament of Liberation* says, 'Should we try to illustrate this triad of misery by similes, that of conditioned existence would be like an unripe fruit.'

W. C. Williams:
>Thus moonlight
>is the perfect
>human touch.   *(Spring and All)*

                                ک

The men's room wall again:
>'This is a nice place. It has good pussy.'

                                ک

>Quod quaerimus publice minimo pretio venditur, et si nosceretur, ne tantillum venderent mercatores.

>The *lapis philosophorum* is *exilis*, unwanted. It is thrown out into the street or onto the dunghill. It is the commonest thing, to be picked up anywhere, *in planitie, in montibus et aquis.*

Notes from Rodeo

We climbed yesterday up a little canyon – early, just after sunrise, parking the pickup at that spot 'near the windmill,' among the islands of tender green scrub mesquite. Mesquite and a few ephedra plants: that's all the drought will let grow, though there were a few struggling flowering shrubs just on the skirts of the range, and one miraculous little pale blue flower.

The canyon went up in a series of huge steps, with bone-dry waterfalls between. The head of it, as we could see after a while, widened out into a rough cirque; actually, the canyon split into two ravines as it approached this height. We joked about finding a little lake up there, laughed over feigned disappointment when there turned out to be none. 'All this way, and there's no water at all!'

Just above where the two ravines parted stood two isolated columns, with between them, part-way up, a ragged connecting bridge. We sat down and looked at them for a while. 'This is what they're doing,' she said, and we touched tongues. I glanced over the area. 'Wish there was a nice sandy place up here where we could make love.' 'Yeah.' We stood up, looked around. I spotted a patch of deep, clean, silvery sand at the foot of a large rock. We carefully laid our shirts out on it. There was even a bench rock, for greater comfort in taking off the boots.

The breeze had the same softness as the canyon shadows. Up around the south side of the cirque, glancing sunlight warmed the rocks, playing on them like music.

The evening Jack Carington shot that Alvarez fellow who was hanging out with him, that was the same day I'd finally gotten the new set of tires for the pickup. When I got back from work I found Ed had thrown the tires in the back of the pickup, so I watered the garden as quick as I could and drove on over to Jack's gas station. Old Man Carington died last winter, so Jack had been running it. He's only about twenty.

When I got there, I found Jack's wife sitting all by herself on a bench in front of the Desert Inn. That's the name of that junk heap of a Conoco station – a tangle of beat-up equipment, scrap, cars with incomprehensible ailments scattered around. Jack's wife must have just about had her baby by now. I don't know, though, because she's gone to stay with some folks in Lordsburg so she can be near Jack. She visits him twice a day, they say. Anyway, she was just sitting there, very quiet, and the setting sun was shining on her. She's a pretty little thing, and she had that invincible glow that a pregnant woman has. She was just beautiful. But her face was sad. She knew darned well she'd made a mistake, marrying Jack. Anyway, I got out and said hello to her. Just then there were two or three shots from out by Jack's father's house, across the Southern Pacific right-of-way. (They took up the tracks years ago.) 'Oh,' she said, 'I hope that Mexican didn't shoot Jack. Jack doesn't have a gun with him.' I didn't fully appreciate the situation, so I said something about that being unlikely. 'I suppose so,' she said; and then, 'Oh, I hate guns.' 'I guess Jack likes guns quite a bit,' I said, not wanting to say, 'Well, you sure married the wrong man.' Jack slings guns around like water pistols. Not long before he'd told me, with his mad, leering grin, that he sometimes shot off pistols even inside the gas station. 'It's good publicity,' he said. 'People like to see the bullet holes in the walls.'

Well, a little later, Jack & that Alvarez (he wasn't really Mexican, he was from San Antonio, but that makes no difference to people around here) showed up and Jack got to work on my tires. And as he worked, he started in on his older brother, Dave.

Dave got shot late one night a year ago by Hank Moreton. Hank was deputy sheriff at the time, having been appointed by some misbegotten process or other. There was some kind of drunken fracas in the bar, with Hank, Jack, and Dave shouting defiance at each other. Later the same night Dave broke into Hank's place. Nobody ever knew exactly what happened, although a persistent rumor had it that Dave was actually shot outside Hank's door, in the back. Hank was acquitted, of course: self-defense. In the meantime, though, he bugged out of Rodeo, fast. He was rightly afraid that Jack, who thought the world of Dave, would kill him.

Jack didn't, though. A handsome, ingratiatingly charming fellow with the emotions of a three year old, he couldn't get it together to do anything more than go find Hank and punch him through a window; and talk. Jack radiates frustration & hate like a short-circuited loudspeaker, but decisive action is beyond him. Anyway, as he was putting on my tires he started in on Dave & Hank, getting more and more drunk with fury. He was like a burning tire (I burn a lot of tires on my job): red flames and rolling billows of filthy black smoke. A true vision of hell. I didn't say much, especially since I knew Hank and up until a couple of weeks ago, when he quit, worked with him here at the truckstop. A crablike human being, a dime-store character disgustingly taking himself for a dragon killer. (And even more disgustingly, many of the good folk of Rodeo seem to agree.) But – these are all men.

So, later that night, Jack shot Alvarez. He called up the sheriff in Lordsburg the next afternoon, himself, to report the event. Said it was self-defense. Down came the sheriff, took lots of pictures & stuff, which, on the way back, he proudly exhibited in the truckstop café. Buzz, buzz, buzz went the talk. People said Jack had driven himself to jail. But no: when I passed his gas station that day on my way back from work, there he was, fooling around at the pumps. A few days later, though, the autopsy report came back from Tucson. Jack claimed he'd shot the guy around noon, but the autopsy showed Alvarez had been shot the night before. Early the next morning they picked Jack up for first-degree murder. If he's tried in Hidalgo County they'll hang him for sure – they'd just love to get rid of him. But I know Jack's lawyer, too. He's going to try to get a change of venue and another judge. He's going to shoot for intentional homicide. First-degree murder is ridiculous, as anyone who knows Jack can see. But, of course, Jack might be better off dead – he's all burnt out and crazy as it is – can't possibly straighten out. In jail, he tied a piece of string around his trigger finger, said he was going to let it drop off so he could never do that again; but they got the string off in time. Everyone in Rodeo agrees that it's his old man who did it to him. Old Ray was about as charming and cussed as they come. As one old timer said, 'Yep, if there were two sides to a question, Ray would always be on the wrong one.'

From a Wintry Northern State

Rodeo will not go unsung.
It is not the mountains near & far,
the clean sweep of the treeless valley,
the delicate colors,
or the endless show of the wide sky.
No, it is space.
Pure tones play against silence.
Even drinking a Dr Pepper with that rogue Lou in his
    Enco station,
the ground is empty.
There are no beings to save.
Say it's sundown.
The shadow of Portal Peak is climbing up into the canyons,
mourning doves are calling,
you're walking home.
Back to the dusty streets 'in town.'
The enchanted world is always there.
No need to remember it or forget it.
Constant, it gives you that priceless gift:
nothing, the field where things move.

Cruising the vast bowl of the heavens
in the first light of dawn
on steady wing,
the winds calm,
the lift perfect,
sustaining the mass
thousands of feet over nothing.
And the ground
not to be touched –
lest one footfall
break the balance, impossible,
of water and fire;
lest earth and oceans sunder
and the great city
in all its perfection
die the great death.
Not one touch.
The calm of morning.

I'm in love again.
The heart clamors to sing.
I would bring up from the deepest place in my body
words to raise the San Simon Valley,
the total landscape,
high in the light:
stretched out, spacious, minutely inhabited –
a world at a glance,
picked out in the keen morning sun.

The words, it's the words above all,
the knots, the leaves,
drifting things,
oddments, a dust of shapes
borne down the swift stream.
You catch them if you can,
breathe with awkward breath upon them,
hoping some will live before they dry –
give your design some lasting hue.
Patterns –
words to clothe patterns in,
to dress the speechless real
in colors gay or somber:
the moving finery
our love delights in, knowing no other way
to say, 'This is your world,
sensible, true;
& whatever is, it is for you.'

How could there be nothing to write?
I stare at the mesh of the tablecloth,
reflecting upon the white thread,
the little knots at each square intersection.
Symbols float into the mind:
Indra's net, the web of existence –
but that's all by way of making conversation.
I talk to myself in grand meanings for a while,
but the tablecloth is the skeleton of it all,
and the constant reminder.
The white threads cross, a white net
big enough to catch nothing in.

Remember ragged May,
no gentle season in that land,
when charged with grit the gales race on
up from the hot south, up the San Simon Valley,
blind, till the mind rattles thoughts like stones.
The windmill chinks and clanks,
the gusts sigh and howl,
dust drifts in through every crack,
of which there are many,
round the window frames, under the door,
or maybe some little hole in the wall
right by your pillow.
It's all from those farms,
that tilled desert soil.
Overhead the clouds have no shape.
The colors are dull.
You can't even depend on the mail
to bring a fresh touch to the morning.
The height of spring in Rodeo
is waiting out the wind.

Will it be enough to evoke the stones?
Will the rest follow?
Will a few boulders scattered in the field,
their butts sunk in earth,
split open
& the soul arise like dawn?
The Lord says,
It's human flesh I'll put on,
walk among the stones
and see how the agave grows;
dig wells too;
keep goats and pigs;
tangle with my neighbor;
haul rocks for walls.
Once the stone splits,
then the real work starts.

Go play among the stones.
The stones?
Can't think of where else to go.
Dusky red stones, pebbled with white or grey.
Into the gravel between them, an ant, tiny plants.
What to do out in this desert?
Anxious, anxious what to do.
Forgetting to breathe.
I lower my gaze to the stones.

Might they turn into bread?
Loaves, rolls, steamed dumplings,
warm masses all yeasty & breathing –
little breads, little heads –
can you make children of them?
Playing among the stones.

It's a cyclical process.
The trouble is, the creation of life is a duty,
not a joy.
That's a trouble, worrying about joy.
I use the word loosely.
I should take the trouble to look more closely.
If I looked closer at the stones I would see that they are what
     they are –
an ingenious notion;
and if I swept my gaze around the horizon
I would see that the far distances are scarier than I expected.
Actually, I might look in the middle ground,
at some rock or spur,
vacantly, absorbed in a babel of thoughts.

Why, why make the stones sing?
To really believe that the earth moves –
struck like a bell, ringing,
singing through space –
why not let them rest.
They sit there so lightly, really,
they belong.
If a lizard sits on a stone, may it not feel secure?
Need a stone be loud, be eloquent?
Let the stones be silent.

Let us listen to something else,
I and the stones.
Wind is blowing through the mesquite,
wind is whistling through the sisals and the agaves –
a lively feel and sound,
far, far sound,
and the look of a few green leaves.

Sitting like a stone,
heavy on the bosom of earth.
Oh to talk with the tongue of stones,
the voice of the dumb.
A silent cry –
reconstructing the memory of rocks,
their fractures and metamorphoses,
eons of tumbling waters –
dry these ten thousand years –
that rounded them a little,
knocked off their angles.
Sitting in place since the last ice age,
the last volcano.
Sun most every morning,
moon most nights;
frost and burning, round and round.
Centuries pass like an unremembered dream.
The agave grows, flowers and passes
from among the stones of the hillside
like the hawk's shadow,
the coyote's footfall,
a stray wolf passing that way,
that, if the world lasts long enough,
may come again.

The senses of stones –
a reaction zone
some molecules thick –
room for conversation
with heat, with light,
with the tingling liquor of air;
soil for the lichens
tickle of ant feet,
rare brush of the stinkbug's shell.

Secret: it isn't the stones that sing,
or the stones that are dumb.
The land rises if you're going that way,
or takes you down to the town.
Now, the town is a small place,
and the people are quite real.
Lloyd sells both nuts and bolts,
but stones are not appreciated.
When you need them, you truck them in
and build them with cement
into a wall.
If you have a garden, you know more than you want to know
about stones.
The stones therefore lie low,
and the singing seems to come from far away.
You might forget about it.
Stones don't sing.
No, and they're not dumb.
It's not specially theirs, the voice
that comes through, that is
as the land rises,
lifts up to a spur
or first round hill
hard to walk on,
thickly strewn with stones –
naked stones, abandoned,
jostling and heaving to a pulse
that moves with the eons;
dense, slow sons
of mountains long since gone,
split off cliffs

that crumbled into this:
a rowdy crowd of random stones,
asleep.

What do you hear? What do you hear?

If the stone won't sing, kick it away.
If it does sing, cover your ears –
and moan and groan at the stifling silence.
Little red beating stone.

I don't want to write a poem.
I don't have to do it.
I'm here, aren't I?
I'm not volunteering.
Just because the book's open –
doesn't mean a thing.
Blank pages?
I've nothing to say, anyway.
Nothing to put down.
Let them stay blank!
That's what the real sutras are:
blank pages.
Let the Emperor be disappointed, not me.

(But think with what love
white paper welcomes in the seeping,
the black, spreading ink.)

I've been out here with the stones so long now,
It's hard not to feel friendly.
Fellow wayfarers on the pathway of life –
of transformation, at least.
It's that, no doubt, that's why we're alive.
But I admit I forget.
And when you forget, it's gone.
You can't just say 'I remember'
and make it so.
It isn't so.
There's the fall.
Me being different from the stones.
This anonymous stone, say.
He has a maddening randomness.
It signals a certain unresponsiveness, no doubt.
What do you say to someone like that?
Is he really my brother?
Still, here we are, out in the desert together.
He's just been here a little longer than I have.
We could talk.
No doubt I should say something to him.

Instead of going to this stone, of course,
I could have him come with me.

It's comforting:
there's always something to say about this stone.
Something to talk about.
A regular conversation piece.
I have it now warm against my body,
inside my jacket.
It's just a stone,
but I value it somehow.
I don't show it to other people.
I warm it on my own.
You'd never think, to look at me,
that I have this stone.

I get up off the gritty ground
and walk around among the weeds and washes.
I think about going home.
Light will soon be failing.
I think the desert is beautiful.
It's all right,
now I have this stone.

It's a smooth stone, of course,
a kind of irregular egg shape,
brownish in color, without flecks or streaks.
Some sort of petrified organ, perhaps.
It is very mute indeed,
but yields somehow to the eye.
Its mass and shape fit well in the hand.
A homey sort of stone.

I will warm this stone of mine.
I will look about me.

I will consider.
They say I could do better,
I could do great things –
but I am waiting, waiting
for the stone to move.
How does a stone move?
I do not know.
I do not know if this stone
will ever move or not;
but it all comes down to that,
that the stone should move.
The process, if there is one,
cannot be hurried;
it is not mine.
I can say the stone is mine,
but not the moving of the stone.
It is that sign
I am waiting for.
I will consider.
I will look about me.
I will see.

The trouble with this doggone stone
is you have to do something with it.
Dispose of it.
And you can't just throw it away, no,
you have to make it turn into something else.
That's the law.
It's in the official records.
Nothing not transmuted will enter heaven.
And the damn thing's yours!
You've got to change it!
You're responsible.
And you don't know what to do.
So you wait.
You wait, hoping something will change.
You don't know how,
but maybe, maybe …

Meanwhile, pythons slide through the brush, the waters of great rivers run, great beasts surge in the steamy heat, and in the trees screech rare birds. Flashes of red and green. Soft fur. Butterflies. Scent of heavy flowers.

Startled –
looking away a second from the stone,
glancing around,
afraid.
There's nothing out there, you say.
Why, that street lamp could eat me.
What of the merciless structure of glass?
The maddened eye?
I think I'd better watch my stone.
Look down.
It isn't real, it isn't real.
Down at the ground.
Pretend I'm busy,
waiting.

The little bird flies, but drifts with every wind that blows.

Poor little stone!
How can it survive in the House of Illusion?
So sapped of substance,
overwhelmed,
it'll shrivel like a raisin
& crumble to dust.
I'll be left with nothing!
Lost!
Nothing to hold onto!
Swept away on the whirling flood!

A little petting & stroking
and it'll be all right.
Keep feeding the little fellow.

Heh, heh.
He don't say nothing, the stone.

You come to a wide place in the road, your mind wanders
        around.
Sauntering about in the new space.
Sniffing and poking,
hands in pockets,
glancing at odd, meaningless things.
A wide place in the stream,
to drift in a while,
moor by the bank,
& dream –
a public square,
vast and formal,
where the eye plays over people walking,
knots of people, single figures,
men & women, hurrying,
and arteries full of cars.
Fountains, an obelisk,
and pigeons, fluttering,
the mind roaming over it all –
a great hall or cathedral,
incense smoke in a haze
drifting through shafts of sunlight.
A wide space
for slow, very easy motion,
all the pull nearly forgotten,
the pull of the road.

I'll take it in my mouth, the stone,
let it melt on the tongue:
matter dissolving
into space, a clear light
without holes or knots.
There's nothing specially vast about vastness;
small things that move are large enough.
What comes in will do,
what goes out leaves things as they are.
For a time the stone is gone,
but as I speak it gathers,
my teeth click against it.
I expel it into my hand,
round inscrutable, hard,
though not unfriendly.
I put it in my pocket again
and stare down the road.

There's a girl in the road,
a little girl,
playing with a turtle.
When the turtle gets frightened,
hides head and legs,
the girl waits patiently
till he comes out again and waddles a step.
Then she picks him up and looks him in the eye,
while his feet wave slowly in the air;
and she puts him down and creeps after him
as he deliberately wanders from the road.

A music from the mountains, low but keen;
a circle of humming.
A chorus unseen of sound more broad,
more plain than men's voices;
a ringing harmony
of things as they are.
Something true.
An actual choir,
the song that no ear misses:
heard now, unhurried,
clear as a bell.

A snake appears in the path.
Let him lie by the stone,
fractured now;
let him range round it.
He will claim it, the snake,
his tongue flickers, he knows.
His scales glide,
his reptile eyes watch.
He appears in the road
and the stone is broken,
as though something suddenly
was born from it.
In an instant while nobody looked,
while the mind blinked,
those hooded eyes came,
likewise the unbearable poise.
Let the creature be.

Let the stone be under sea.
How shall we fish?
Calling, calling out over the waves,
the tossing face of the waters.
Calling: Come back, come back!
Come, my Lord, up from the deep,
to rest in my hand, perfect;
calling out into the wind,
into the cries of gulls,
the rushing air,
Come, my love, come to me,
bright my bright, bright love to me –
Ah, that face the waters show:
to break it, to dive
down into the dark sea,
sliding down to the cold, the still
where no one can come,
to the ground where my love hides,
bright in the dragon shrine –
the honored captive –
to seize, to bear up,
the body bursting…

My lady whose robe is heaven,
whose limbs are trees in leaf,
whose gifts are fruit,
perfected, full
with light for all who eat,
turn, turn, I pray,
through sun and moon
this stone I hold into a pearl,
to be my gift to thee.

Peer into a jar:
what do you see?
A space apart,
complete, fully alive.
The same world could all be in there,
exquisitely fine,
showing how arbitrary are our notions of scale.
Is my world absolutely larger than a jar?
The same world?
Voices in the jar's inner wall
shout across that space,
far, far out into the distance,
talking over light years
amongst themselves.
Galaxies dance and swim.
And sometimes it's like a quiet gathering,
talking easily and low.
The glaze shines in the light.
I put my hand inside.
What of me is the guest, and what the host?

A great valley under the stars,
the ground still,
shapes of mountains dark on the dark sky;
four thousand miles straight down,
unimaginable,
the heart without light of the whole earth's mass.
Brushing the skin, a light wind
rises, stiff weeds rustle and sing.
The stones feel:
lichens' slow sucking and prying,
sharp bite of frost,
splitting heat,
eon by eon flaking and feeding
creatures delicate, each in its place:
the tide-reaches
between magma and space.

These are some things I think about.
And I was going to show you a storm
rushing through, or a great burning
flexing and cracking the boulders;
plant skeletons bouncing and rolling;
and how all this passes
just like the most perfect autumn day.

But you know all this as well as I, or as poorly.
I would seize the heart from this mineral body
to give you, unencumbered,
in your infinite person,
but in the end do not know how.
And the great valley under the stars, too,
breathes with the planet's fine, slow breath

in my imagination —
one of my bodies, perhaps, but not the one
compounded of water and ash.
Say it's an angel,
or a shewing
of the Holy Immovable Lord.
But my own flesh clings to this heart
and imposes upon it strictures.
I speak of high things but am not heaven.
This you know too;
and, incarnate as you are after all,
I know you the same;
and neither knows yet, in and of the other, the workings of it.
Not to trust you, though, is beyond me;
and I will be as upright as I can.
I am speaking to you already,
though haltingly.
I have a notion where we are,
though I could be wrong.
But it's true at least we're on earth
and that earth is our home.
We have met — no small thing;
and we will be together as we may.

SHE

   if one sleeps in a black-draped room
      do shadows fall across brite dreams?
   if one dreams in the night
     do the colors fade?

SHE

I fear the view thru colored glass
& the desire for gold
but not to look into the rainbow –
what colors I will wear
what mist & sun combine

SHE

you dream –
& I lean into yr dream
with mine
the same
sweet spring of union

HE

She had asked, Is anything new with you?

        No, nothing new,
        for winter lies in rags while spring
        barely stirs; I dream
        of substance power might give
        our airy love.

HE

Again, light star flowers
sweeping on airy breath
to earth: winter's show
over a world inert
I dream I move.

SHE

I stood at a window onto twilight (my home
returning birds, a wind, a crescent moon)
I wld give you yr kingdom
I wld fly to you and dress myself in rainbows.

SHE

tho I offer you a flower cup
filled with wine
it is so light – will you forget?
such an intrusion
on your sobriety

HE

Am I that sober?

    Light the cup is, yes,
    and light the love,
    but thorough. This your flower
    opens into all my world –
    shall I forget?

    On what sobriety of mine
    would you intrude?
    Before you ever knew you offered wine,
    your cup had touched my lips
    with sage intoxication.

Love, I dreamed you moved
into my house. This morning
in the hall I knew you there
behind that door, asleep,
filling with dear breath my empty room.

So we start our second winter,
you and I –
oh those walks through the cold and the snow to you,
and all the poems!

In half light we pause
for our last words, shy
yet drawn, at polite distance;
flame through my eyes leaps
unbidden to bathe you in fire.

A round, black, lustrous dish made by Maria of San Ildefonso:
the center shines like a dark moon, and around the rim coils
a dragon. A lightning arrow darts from the dragon's mouth.

> I roll forth at ease
> through tumbling clouds,
> glance down:
> below, in the lordly forest,
> a tree bursts into flame.

Song

My lady, you are a dark range
alive with clean, prism colors,
rainbows or butterfly wings, bright gleams
with mass, shifting
as night snow falls
over a spacious landscape,
rushing and eddying, curling and yielding,
flake by flake
to the minutely detailed touch of the invisible wind.
You are a landscape of light,
you are a shadow
doubling each movement of body or spirit.
You are the sum of all correspondences,
the dancing echo I dance to.

A hollow reed sounds in the great sky;
the frozen lake streams with restless snow.
White and black he walks the open ice.
Clouds range like nations down the wind.

www.ingramcontent.com/pod-product-compliance
Lightning Source LLC
Chambersburg PA
CBHW031212090426
42736CB00009B/879